W9-AYO-563

BARNYARD LULLABY

FRANK ASCH

ALADDIN PAPERBACKS

New York   London   Toronto   Sydney   Singapore

One night, when the barnyard was quiet,
Mother Hen began to sing.
To the farmer in his bed her song sounded like
so much cluck, **cluck, clucking.**

But her chicks heard the music
and understood the words.
To them it was a beautiful lullaby
that went like this:

Gather round, my children,
Cuddle as I sing,
Let yourselves grow sleepy,
Safe beneath my wing.
Close your eyes, my darlings,
Let your cares drift away.
Go to sleep, my sweethearts,
Tomorrow is a brand-new day.

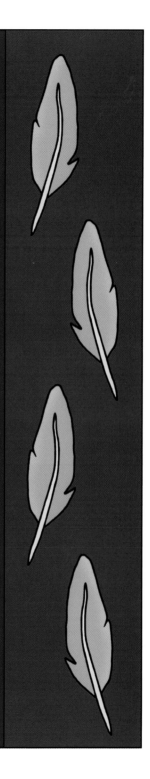

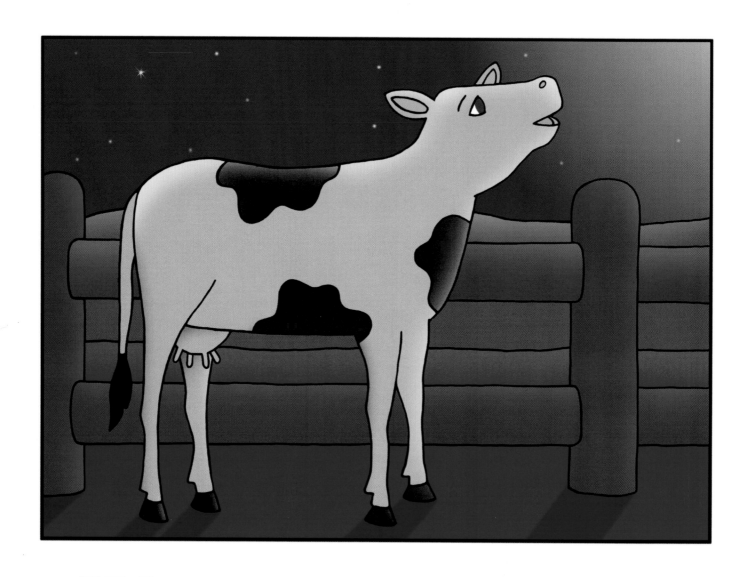

W hat a lovely song," thought Mother Cow, and she too began to sing.
To the farmer in his bed her song sounded like so much moo, **moo, mooing.**

But her calf heard the music
and understood the words.
To him it was a beautiful lullaby
that went like this:

Come lie beside me
Under stars so bright.
Let dreams of shady pastures
Bring on the morning light.
Close your eyes, my darling,
Let your cares drift away.
Go to sleep, my sweetheart,
Tomorrow is a brand-new day.

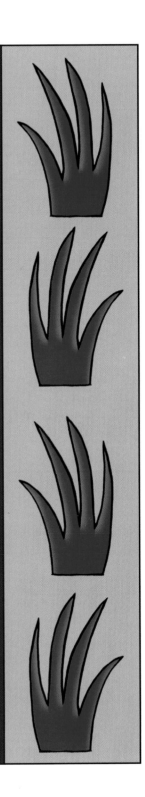

W hat a lovely song," thought Mother Horse, and she too began to sing.
To the farmer in his bed her song sounded like so much neigh, neigh, **neighing.**

But her colt heard the music
and understood the words.
To him it was a beautiful lullaby
that went like this:

Tuck your legs beneath you,
Legs that love to run.
Feel them growing ever stronger.
Let the day be done.
Close your eyes, my darling,
Let your cares drift away.
Go to sleep, my sweetheart,
Tomorrow is a brand-new day.

W hat a lovely song," thought Mother Pig, and she too began to sing.
To the farmer in his bed her song sounded like so much oink, oink, oinking.

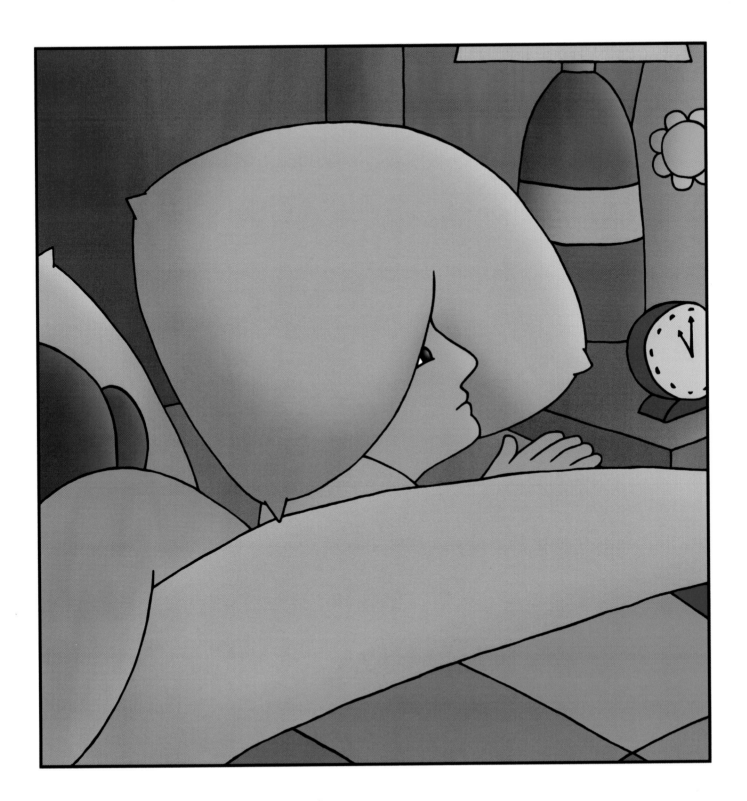

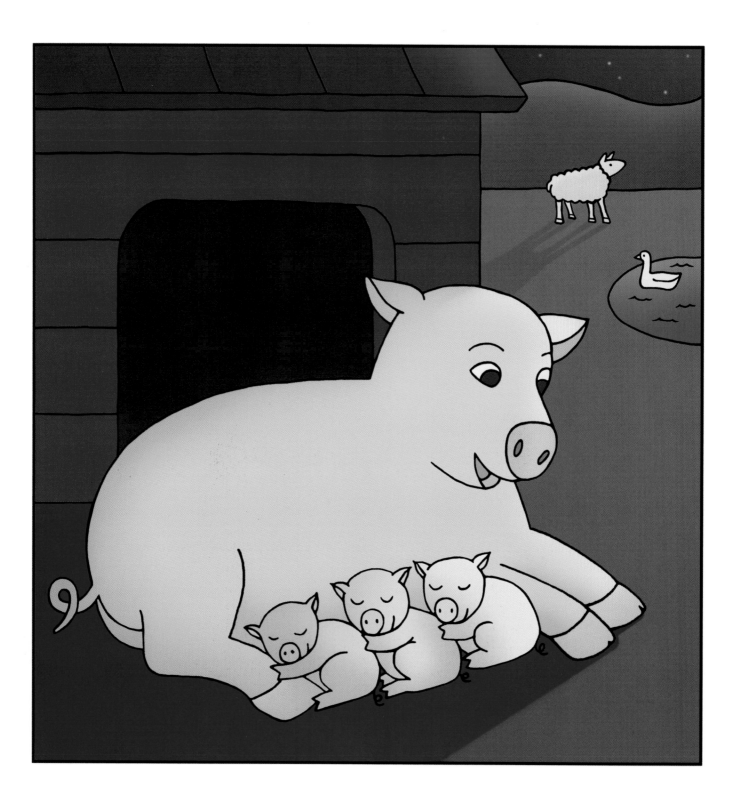

But her piglets heard the music
and understood the words.
To them it was a beautiful lullaby
that went like this:

Wallowing in puddles,
Squealing with delight,
You've all had your mud bath,
Now it's time to say good night.
Close your eyes, my darlings,
Let your cares drift away.
Go to sleep, my sweethearts,
Tomorrow is a brand-new day.

W hat a lovely song," thought Mother Sheep, and she too began to sing.
To the farmer in his bed her song sounded like so much baa, **baa, baaing.**

But her lamb heard the music
and understood the words.
To her it was a beautiful lullaby
that went like this:

You danced in the clover,
While we grazed upon the hill.
Make my wool your pillow,
Let it keep you from the chill.
Close your eyes, my darling,
Let your cares drift away.
Go to sleep, my sweetheart,
Tomorrow is a brand-new day.

"Oh, what a lovely song," thought Mother Goose, and she too began to sing.
To the farmer in his bed her song sounded like so much honk, **honk, honking.**

But her goslings heard the music
and understood the words.
To them it was a beautiful lullaby
that went like this:

Waddle from the pond, dears,
To our downy nest.
Swimming, dunking all the day,
Goslings need a rest.
Close your eyes, my darlings,
Let your cares drift away.
Go to sleep, my sweethearts,
Tomorrow is a brand-new day.

While the baby animals listened to their mothers' sweet voices, all the farmer heard was so much clucking and mooing and neighing and oinking and baaing and honking.
So he hollered out the window, "BE QUIET!"
But that only woke up his own baby, who started to cry. "WAAAAAAA!"

"Now look what you've done!"
grumbled the farmer's wife,
and she began to sing:

Gentle breezes blowing
Softly in your hair.
Sounds of nighttime calling,
Music in the air.
Close your eyes, my darling,
Let your cares drift away.
Go to sleep, my sweetheart,
Tomorrow is a brand-new day.

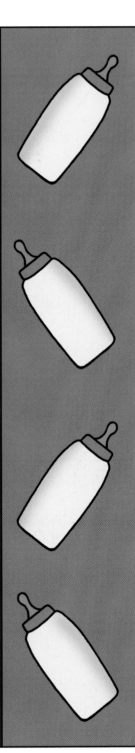

To the animals in the barnyard
her song was just so much noise.
But the farmer heard the music
and understood the words.
To him it was a beautiful lullaby.

To Jenny and Malindi

First Aladdin Paperbacks edition April 2001

Text and illustrations copyright © 1998 by Frank Asch

Aladdin Paperbacks
An imprint of Simon & Schuster Children's Publishing Division
1230 Avenue of the Americas
New York, NY 10020

All rights reserved, including the right of reproduction in whole or in part in any form.

Also available in a Simon & Schuster Books for Young Readers hardcover edition

Designed by Anahid Hamparian
The text for this book was set in 22-point Life.
The illustrations were rendered in Photoshop.

Printed in Hong Kong
10 9 8 7 6 5 4 3 2 1

The Library of Congress has cataloged the hardcover edition as follows:

Asch, Frank.
Barnyard lullaby / by Frank Asch.
p.   cm.
Summary: Although the farmer only hears animal noises, when the different barnyard animals sing lullabies to their
respective children, the babies understand the words. Includes music.
ISBN: 0-689-81363-5 (hc.)
1. Children's songs—United States—Texts. [1. Domestic animals—Songs and music. 2. Animal sounds—Songs and music.
3. Lullabies. 4. Songs.] I. Title.
PZ8.3.A7Bar 1998 782.42'1582—dc21 [E] 96-44987
ISBN: 0-689-84256-2 (Aladdin pbk.)

BARNYARD LULLABY

WORDS BY FRANK ASCH **MUSIC BY MELISSA CHESNUT**

To hear what the lullaby sounded like to the farmer, try singing this with some friends.
Each person can learn a different animal's part; when all the parts are sung together,
you'll understand why the farmer needed some QUIET!

CHORUS

Close your eyes, my dar - ling(s), Let your cares drift a - way.

Go to sleep, my sweet - heart(s), To - mor - row is a brand - new day.

1. HEN

Gath - er round, my child - ren, Cud - dle as I sing,

Let your - selves grow sleep - y, Safe be - neath my wing.

2. COW

Come lie be - side me Un - der stars so bright.

Let dreams of shad - y pas - tures Bring on the morn - ing light.